# Rain of Thoughts

## Poems and short stories
## by Anthony Goulet

I don't write because I think I have the answers. I write because I am willing to learn.

Creator,

Help us to think what You want us to think and how You want us to think it.

Help us to see what You want us to see and how You want us to see it.

Help us to hear what You want us to hear and how You want us to hear it.

Help us to say what You want us to say and how You want us to say it.

Help us to feel what You want us to feel and how You want us to feel it.

Help us to do what You want us to do and how You want us to do it.

For too long we have struggled in search of what we want without You. We return to You now, and we thank You for restoring our holy minds as we think with You. We thank You for raining Your holy thoughts upon us so that we think, see, hear, say, feel, and do only that which is in alignment with Your love.

Amen

# This Holy Instant

Originally Published in Elephant Journal

On the mountaintop, upon the altar of light he was born. Others recognized him as the love he is and the love he came from. In his innocence others were able to see their own innocence again, and recall what truly matters. He was a precious child. Wherever he was people wanted to hold him because he wasn't heavy, he was light because he was love. When people held him they held a holy reminder of the truth of what we are.

As time went by the boy grew into a young man. In his journey from infancy to being a young man he encountered those who recognized him as the love he is. He also encountered others who saw him completely different than the love is. Those who couldn't recognize him as the love he is gave him a bag to carry. He was instructed to use the bag in this manner: *Place everything you say, do, and think that is wrong in this bag and carry it.* Those who recognized him as the love he is also handed him a bag to carry with this instruction: *Place everything you say, do, and think that is right in this bag and carry it.*

Accepting the bags and the instructions, he went on his life journey. Every day, whether at work or play, either he or someone else placed something in each of his bags. Some days his bag of wrong was heavier than his bag of right; and other days his bag of right was much lighter than his bag of wrong. He was strong, so he easily compensated from one side to the other to walk balanced and straight in public. However, every evening in private he unpacked both bags before going to bed. As he looked through his bag of wrong, he cried and condemned himself; and as he looked through his bag of right, he smiled, boasted, and congratulated himself. Placing all of his rights and wrongs back in their appropriate bags, he would sleep. Some nights when he forgot to place his wrongs in their appropriate bag, sleeping proved to be difficult.

Days passed, merging with weeks, blending to years, and accumulated to decades of the rights and wrongs he and others gave him to carry about himself. He began to lose his balance, even in public. Both bags were full and heavy, overflowing onto others in every interaction. Some moments his wrongs, along with the inferiority and condemnation that comes with that bag, spilled onto others. In other moments his rights, along with a sense of superiority and self-righteous indignation that comes with that bag, spilled onto others. Weary, frustrated, and lost, he decided to return to the mountain where he was born in hopes of finding himself.

Hours after sunset he finally made the seventeen-inch journey from his head to his heart, and was once again upon the mountaintop where he was born. He didn't have to light a fire, because the star that never moves from that special place illuminated the entire area with its light. His grip loosened from the heavy bags of wrong and right as the memory of who he is ran through his tears, and spilled upon the altar of light where he was born. His tears reflected the light that

has always shone brightly upon the altar of his heart,
cleansing it, and revealing an inscription:

In this Holy instant
Of Light and Love you were born
And Light and Love you will always be
Place your bags of rights and wrongs
On either side of me

Step back upon the altar
Where light never ceases
And allow the light of love
To dissolve the useless pieces
Pieces of rights or wrongs
Hold not one glimpse of you
Step back upon this altar
To remember all that's true

You are not lost
You've just used your eyes to see
Only your bags of rights and wrongs
Exchanging holy memory for misery

You're not in either bag
And cannot be found in one or both
No matter if you hate yourself
Or use each day to boast

Beyond failures or successes
Past confidence or guesses
Afar from gracefulness or messes
Is your true reflection – Love

Of Light and Love you were born
And Light and Love you'll always be
Throughout your life you may come here heavy
Yet in this holy instant you are free

# Stop Thinking You're Not Me

I wear my emotions on my face
For all the world to see
Leading with my chin is easy
At least it is for me

I'm not a strategist playing chess
With you nor anyone else
I unlocked and share
What was once hidden
With the courage to lay it out

So upon this table where we meet
That separates you and me
I open my heart upon it
For both of us to be free

If you lay your heart out, too
Separation will dissolve
Together we'll have the answers
That separation couldn't solve

But in a world of broke and weary
A madman I'm considered to be
Because I share my heart
And all that's within me
Wanting everyone to be free
From what closes our hearts, tears us apart
And makes you think you're not me

# Our Humanity

When we witness a child run into a busy street
When we see an accident about to happen
When we see a baby who is about to fall
When we see a wounded animal
When we see these things
Something overtakes us
It pulls us towards where help is needed
It's the most natural instinct of our soul – our spirit
A place of purity with no thought of separation
No thought of race, nationality, religion, or politics
A pull to save, serve, and comfort
We are created with it
We are created in it
It is us
Our love for all life
It
Is
Our
Humanity

# It is

It will not command you because it is not arrogant

It will not demand you because it is not controlling

It will not defeat you because it does not attack

It will simply remind you that you are it

It

Is

Love

# Tightropes We Never Had to Walk

Playing chicken with myself

Knowing neither one of us would ever give up

You can't out-dysfunction yourself

Whatever level you want to take it to

will be matched and elevated

There's no room for bluffing

All cards get shown eventually

so eventually we show all our cards

No more wheeling and dealing

Because sometimes what needs to be dealt with

never is

And there's no more wheeling when we let go

of the wheel

Because we see the light or feel the heat from it

As we look at God from a tightrope

We never had to walk

We fall back in His loving arms

Remembering we didn't create ourselves

So there's no point in trying to kill

What is a part of the Great One

Because it can never die, only transition

So we learn to do some of that transitioning here

As we fall from tightropes

We never had to walk

We fall more deeply in love with God, ourselves

and all of creation

When we let go and fall back into grace

From tightropes we never had to walk

# Runners Not Knowing Why

Some people will push you away
No matter what you say or do
Running after them only leaves you left again
And when two people who push others away
Embrace one another
It's a strange dance that begins and ends
On the starting line
Neither of them saying it, but they're both waiting
For the sound of the starting pistol
To outrun the other in a lonely race of isolation
That has no finish line
All the while they long for what they ran from
But won't stop running
As if the blasts from starting pistols
Drown out the cries of those who love them
Calling them back from isolation
But they never feel at home
They're runners
And those who aren't runners are tortured
But not nearly as much as those
who are always running
Not knowing why

# You Appeared

Your being vibrates with sacred tones –
Sounds of love that created you
A spark of beginning in a word!
Then you appeared

# When It's Not Just a Flesh Wound

The cuts, scars, scrapes
Broken bones, stitches, casts, and tape
Impermanence like paper and pen
It's just a flesh wound

Sores disappeared
Scars evidence of healing
Casts taken off
Stitches taken out
It's just a flesh wound

Many sit with us all night
Caring for wounds visible by sight
Strangers, acquaintances, family, and friends
When it's just a flesh wound

Who dares to respond to the wounds of the spirit?
Who doesn't run when the heart breaks?
Who in comfortable silence is present
When your soul shakes?

When it's not just a flesh wound
what number do you call?

What name written in light
appears upon the darkness of your mind's wall?

Light will always change darkness
Darkness can never change light
A warrior rises killing pain with presents of presence

Warriors rise because warriors love
Not knowing the meaning of conditional,
a warrior is there
Giving safe emergency rooms
where tears can freely flow
Performing open heart surgery
on hearts closed from being exposed
to pain, loss, and tragedy

Removing the blockages
Bypassing the lies
Finding a cure in the obscure
Antidotes for any poison given
Making the meaningless meaningful

The truth doesn't hurt
The lies do
The lies that say you are anything less

than a miracle, blessing, and gift
are untrue

The warrior's surgical toolbox of prayer filled with
Love
Words
Silence
Presence
Song

Warriors remind us to find ourselves
within each other
Love gift wrapped in an earth robe
A true human *being*

Don't be confused because you see!
Remember what rose within those warriors for you
So you can rise as the warrior you are created to be
When it's not just a flesh wound

# Forgiveness and

If you still have an enemy

After you've forgiven your enemy

Then you haven't

Forgiven

Your

Enemy

# Your Highest Calling

You will always recognize your highest calling
by one key trait:

That which fills you

When

You

Give

It

Away

# Offering Only Love

Perceptions are not facts
They're mirrors
Reflecting fear, guilt, sin, blame
Or
Love, innocence, forgiveness, freedom
Love and fear
Are both limitless
Love is limitless in healing
fear is limitless in destruction

Sometimes all the windows in our glasshouses
Need to be broken
So the light can shine through
Revealing the absurdity
That there was a time we saw each other
As anything less
Than sacred blessings, miracles, and gifts
With nothing left to attack or defend
We put down our swords and shields
Offering only love again
and again and again

# God speak

The sword covering your lips makes me wonder
If you're protecting the sacredness of your soul
Or if it's your tongue piercing through your lips

Your tongue, once a sacred flower
Used only for God speak
Turned to hardened steel
Reflecting a heart turned cold
And if your heart has turned cold
Know that one burning ember of love
Remains in the furnace of your heart

It's a spark you cannot destroy
It's a spark that cannot destroy you
It's the spark that created you
It's the spark that *is* you
And using the wind
Of your breath
You can fan it

With one word of remembrance
From the infinite ember of love
Within the fireplace of your heart

Spoken from your spark

Fans the eternal ember back to a blazing fire

Melting cold steel, reigniting the love you are

Resurrecting your tongue from the coldness of death

Back to the warmth of life

Returning you to you -

The beautiful flower

of God speak

You are

# The Sacred Bundle of Light

Originally published in The Good Men Project

It was a time of great difficulty for the people. There were wars, rumors of wars, famine, unwholesome reasoning, unskillful desires, contrived malice, drugs, alcohol, and a thick fog of hopelessness that began to take over the land. It was a time when many no longer believed in their own voice, so they couldn't believe in the voices of others. The people wanted things to be different, yet they attacked all those who thought or acted differently. It was a dark time when rumors, gossip and other forms of violence held the people's attention; while talk of peace, healing, and solutions were mocked. Warriors were perceived as cowards. Cowards were perceived as warriors. Drugs, alcohol, and jealousy were treated as friends, yet friends were treated as enemies.

In the midst of this great despair many cried out to the Creator for help. Since no prayer ever goes unheard or unanswered the Creator sent help immediately. The Creator sent a sacred woman to the people. The sacred woman carried a sacred bundle that was to be gifted to the world. The sacred bundle of light she carried contained the answers to prayers, and memories of what we are, so that we could once again see ourselves and one another as sacred.

The sacred woman's journey from the heavens was a much shorter trip than the journey she took after she arrived on earth. Once on earth the sacred woman had to endure many things on her journey to deliver the sacred bundle to the people. Before the sacred woman was given the sacred bundle to carry and deliver to the people, she was first given the highest possible levels of fortitude and resiliency. She was met with the violence of those difficult times. She suffered through many disappointments, attacks, betrayals, and condemnation. The bundle was given to her to deliver to the people because the Creator knew that although she may feel pain, and she may stumble, she would not be detoured by the mental, physical, and emotional violence that erupted upon the land during those days. She was charged with delivering the bundle of light, so the darkness of those times held not even the slightest chance of victory over her.

Just as the Creator had done for her, she did the same for the bundle. She placed all that she is within the sacred bundle before delivering it to the people. Through the sacred woman, life, fortitude, resilience, and answers to the prayers of the people were all wrapped lovingly inside the bundle of light.

Coming close to death the sacred woman delivered the answers the people cried out for. She laid down her life to deliver the sacred bundle the Creator sent through her. The sacred woman is your mother. The sacred bundle of light the Creator delivered through her to this world is you.

# The First Step is Always Purification

There was a young man who had made many mistakes, but he wanted his life to be better. He wanted something different, positive and good. He wanted to smile again. The young man approached an older man who he knew had made many of the same mistakes as him. The young man asked the older man, "I know you've made many of the same mistakes I have made and now your life is good. You're living positive and helping others. You smile a lot. I want that. I want my life to be good. I want to live positively and help others. I want to smile again. How do I do that?"

The older man smiled, "The first step is always purification. First, go to God and pour your heart out to Him. Ask God to purify you, cleanse you, and put all the broken pieces together to make you whole again. Ask God to take you back to your heart to remember and reclaim your vision, dreams, and purpose."

Looking discouraged, the younger man said, "Well, I guess my life isn't going to change anytime soon because it's been many years since I've spoken with God. I've made too many mistakes to approach God right now."

The older man smiled brightly and asked the young man, "Do you go to the soap when your hands are clean or when your hands are dirty?"

"When my hands are dirty," the young man replied. As soon as the young man spoke those words he smiled again and went on his way to have a long overdue conversation with his Maker.

# Love Didn't Teach You That

Bravo!

You know how to hurt someone

Bravo!

Were those skills honed at church?

At ceremony?

Were the teachings of hurting others taught to you

by the Jesus you claim to follow?

The prophet's teachings you claim to know?

The ceremonial leaders you claim to listen to?

Your own heart?

Your own soul?

No!

None of them taught you to hurt others

Hurt taught you to hurt

Then justify hurting others because you're hurting

Yet I'm hurting, too, and I refuse to follow

hurt's teachings

Because I don't want to ever forget

Who I am within you

And who we are within God

There is nothing worse we can do to someone

Who has disconnected from the love they are

When they follow hurt's teachings

Sometimes the best we can do is allow hurt to teach us

What *not* to do

And then draw closer to the warm healing fire

Standing with love -

Our one true Spiritual teacher

Selah!

# Count Your Scars as the Number of Times You've Been Healed, not Wounded

Originally published in The Good Men Project

We have all experienced the bites of betrayal, deceit, and disappointment. Unfortunately, we will experience those bites again throughout this human existence. The bite is razor sharp and lasts less than a second. Our human bodies have been endowed with the ability to heal themselves, and there are often no visible scars from these bites. So why do so many die from a bite that lasts less than a second and heals so quickly? Why is it that some people die to their own passions, callings, trust, compassion, heart, dreams, and potential from a one second bite of betrayal, deceit, or disappointment? Because it is never the bite that kills us, it's the venom.

The cause of death is from the venom entering our being, coursing through our veins, our lives, and inevitably through the lives of all those around us. The venom produces fangs and an aggression within the carrier that makes them ready to bite others because they think this will protect them from being bit again. The venom and fangs of distrust, hate, arrogance, unworthiness, addictions, self-righteousness, contrived malice, self-sabotage, greed, suicide, and violence in all its forms are only some of the things that manifest from venom left within us. This type of poisoned mindset, probably because it has been happening for so long now, is an almost accepted and even expected form of existence. Some may even attempt to convince us that growing fangs and infecting others with poison before others can do that to us is strong, but it isn't. It requires a lot of energy and effort, but not strength. It does, however, require great strength and courage to break a venomous mindset and cycle by seeking the antidote. And those who have dared to embark upon the journey of breaking negative cycles will always find the antidote, because it is available to everyone, but for the antidote to work it must be accepted.

The heart of a person infected with venom begins to shut down and this stage is known as *Don't talk. Don't tell. Don't feel.* Which are the three rules in all unhealthy relationships. Yet, the exact opposite of these rules is required to dissolve the fangs that have grown from the venom. *Talking, telling,* and *feeling* has to happen for the antidote to be accepted. We can talk, tell, and feel with another person, group, or by ourselves in prayer and meditation. We can talk, tell, and feel through writing, painting, drawing, dancing, or in whatever manner we are comfortable, so long as we do it. It doesn't matter how long or how many times we have to talk, tell, and feel, it takes as long as it takes, and individual time frames are different, but the results do not vary. The end results are always the same when we talk, tell, and feel - the fangs dissolve and a newfound desire to heal is uncovered.

With a new inspiration to heal from talking, telling, and feeling, the fangs are dissolved and the aggression is dulled, but the fangs and aggression will regrow if we do not completely eliminate the venom from our being. Talking, telling, and feeling now have to be coupled with an understanding that *facing the truth and finding peace has nothing to do with blame.* Although blame appears logical, blame takes the painful moments in our lives and turns them into the rest of our lives. So, am I saying that someone who bit us and infected us with venom is not at fault? No, but I am saying that it is our responsibility (response-ability) to seek and accept the antidote to the venom from that bite for ourselves. *For as long as our life is someone else's fault, it's not our life.* Do we want our life back, or do we want to stay with the seemingly logical, yet costly path of blame for the rest of our life? Before we consider f.e.a.r - *forget everything and run* back to the comfort zone of blame, let's look at the perspectives of two prominent human beings on the venom of anger and resentment, which are of course impossible to carry without blame. As seemingly logical as blame may be, Buddha and Nelson Mandela offer perspectives that show us the illogical course of blame.

*"Holding on to anger is like grasping a hot coal with the intent of throwing it at someone else; you are the one who gets burned."~ Buddha*

*"Resentment is like drinking poison and then hoping it will kill your enemies."~ Nelson Mandela*

To willingly hold anger and resentment, knowing that anger and resentment will hurt and hinder us, shows us that when we use the tool of blame, we will always blame ourselves. We must have blamed ourselves at some level or we would not be willing to grasp hot coals or drink poison. To put it another way, *we will always receive what we offer, and we can only offer what we carry.*

The antidote is forgiveness. Think about some things you have deemed as unforgivable. Now, ask yourself if there are people who have forgiven what you have deemed as unforgivable. Being honest with ourselves we find that forgivable and unforgivable are boxes that we place things in. To forgive or be unforgiving is but a choice. A simple choice? No. Forgiveness is a choice many never make due to not understanding that blame is self-harm, while forgiveness is the highest act of self-love we can offer ourselves by giving it to others. Understanding that blame is self-harm and forgiveness is self-love moves us from saying *they don't deserve my forgiveness* to *I deserve forgiveness and all its benefits*.

Does this mean we forgive, rid ourselves of the venom we carried for so long, then invite venom carriers over for dinner? No. Forgiveness does not mean we allow people with ill intentions in our lives, or live without healthy boundaries. Healthy boundaries are necessary, and we are able to develop the healthiest boundaries for ourselves when we forgive.

Forgiveness is viewed by many as illogical. Blame, although viewed by many as logical, is a cycle of venom that is insane, hurtful, self-harming, and imprisoning. It took me many years of sampling various remedies, yet when I was introduced to the illogical antidote of forgiveness there was not one single part of my life that was left uncured, unhealed, or undelivered from the venom of pain, loss, tragedy, and fear. I would rather have a so-called illogical antidote that works than a so-called logical remedy that only exacerbates the pain.

If you breath in courage and trust, then say with all your heart, mind, and spirit that you forgive _____(say their names) for _____(say the acts), and allow the tears of purification to rise from within you, pushing out the venom that was never yours to carry, the venom will flow out of you through your tears, our natural purification system. Hold nothing back, let it all out, and you will experience the miracle of forgiveness. You will experience the peace and joy you had before you were bitten, realizing that unforgiveness was blocking you from what we all long for, peace. After forgiving, you will count your scars as the number of times you've been healed, not wounded.

# The Last Words

They talked and talked

Until one day, they couldn't talk anymore

The last words they heard, read, or wrote

was a question:

If you couldn't speak for the rest of your life,
what would the rest of your life speak about you?

# On the Shore of Memories

Memories clinging
Drops of light
Searching for what used to be
On the shore of memories

At times I'm a stowaway
On ships that no longer sail
Hiding below
On the shore of memories

When the tide rises
Sometimes it rocks me to sleep
Other times it rocks me awake
And I cast away
From the shore of memories

Awakened
I allow love's current to take me
Leaving memories on the shore
To make new ones
With those who aren't a memory
So they can smile
When I am

# God's Seed

A seed and all that's within it manifests

Because it gives itself entirely to the earth

When we give ourselves entirely to God's love

The greatness within us manifests


As the seed and all that's within it

Never stops needing the earth

We never stop needing God

# The Gift

Quick!

Give it all away

Before it's all taken

And

No

Longer

A

Gift

# I'll Be There

Those who give everything
Are asked to give more
More than everything

And when givers give their last breath
Takers feed upon what's left

Vampires calling givers selfish
For needing to eat, sleep and cry

When the givers go
The takers too late see
They couldn't take anything from the givers
Because it was given freely

Yes they're around when you need them
They drop everything
Yet when they need you,
well?

Hey, whatever your thing is
I'm sure you're right
You wouldn't have it any other way

I threw my heart out to the world
It was brought back to me
Or maybe the world threw my heart out
And I had to find it
Either way

I've learned I receive what I give
And what I withhold from others
is withheld from me

So give all to all to have all
If you dare

But no matter your decisions
When you need me
I'll be there

# The Sacred Rite of Birth:
# A Ceremony Men Need to Remember

Originally published in the Good Men Project

It's hard to imagine that someone can hate a person who saved their life. We hear so many stories about organ donor recipients who keep in touch with the family of the organ donor out of immense gratitude. We hear other stories about the heroic efforts of a police officer, or brave civilian who saved the life of someone. There is usually a touching reunion that takes place between the survivor and the hero. We hear of combat veterans who continue lifelong bonds that are beyond words due to saving one another's lives in battlefields that only the veterans truly understand.

Apart from sociopaths, relationships at the most intimate level are what we all crave. Everyone wants an intimacy that is beyond words, with a knowing that our heart and the heart of another is connected. If we are blessed to have such a relationship, how could we possibly hate it? More importantly, since we all have this relationship, why do some hate it and everything that reflects it?

Yes, you read correctly, we all have this relationship. We have life, and that is because of a life-giver, a woman, our mothers. And yes, some men hate women. The hatred manifests in many forms, from physical violence, to more subtle forms of violence equally filled with hate, such as women earning less in wages for the same work as men. Regardless how this hatred manifests, it must be addressed and eradicated from the thought systems of humanity for humanity to become fully humane.

Men, we must look within our hearts to remember our manhood; but we have to look towards women to remember our humanity. The sacred life-givers, the women, they were the first to lay down their lives for us, thus they are the first warriors. They never promised they would do it, they just did it, and so their courage cannot be questioned. Men, we have been afforded an opportunity to utilize the gifts waiting to be birthed from us, only because of the warriors who birthed us. Men, the way we treat women shows how we think and feel about the Creator and ourselves. Far too many men demonstrate hate towards the Creator, life, and themselves by disrespecting, using, and abusing women. Any thoughts, feelings, or actions of hatred towards or about women are literally a hatred for life.

Our birthrights are given to us through *the sacred rite of birth*. *The sacred rite of birth* is a ceremony that all women have been charged to lead. Until this ceremony and the leaders of this ceremony are honored, we as men not only negate our manhood and warriorship, we've turned our backs on our humanity and God.

Men, turn back to the warriorship that's within your hearts, and remember the great love that carried you for nine months. Even if you never saw your mother after your birth, is not the moment of your birth, where your mother came so close to death for you to have life, enough to honor her and all other life-givers for the rest of your life?

Within the nine-month ceremony of *the sacred rite of birth* men who abuse women knew a truth that they forgot*: You are a miracle, blessing, and gift.* This truth was known by you when you were curled up within your mother's womb with your ear gently pressed against your heart as you listened to your holy instructions. As the waves of life pulsated around you through your mother's heartbeat, the voice of the sacred synched your heart with all life, giving you your original voice that pulsated *God is-Love is-God is-Love is.* Your original voice has not ceased singing this holy song bestowed upon you through your mother while safe in the womb, but men who abuse women have stopped listening. You were safe within your mother's womb, and women should be safe after you are outside of the womb. Your original, holy instructions continue to beat in perfect rhythm waiting for your return to your original voice. It is such a short walk from your head back to your heart, only seventeen inches, yet without remembering *the sacred rite of birth* the path cannot be found, because when you forget *the sacred rite of birth* there is no light.

We, all men, were once within the holiest place on earth, and when we remember *the sacred rite of birth*, the path to our heart is illuminated, and we know our holy instruction is to recreate that holy place of safety and love on this earth. Remembering *the sacred rite of birth* is perhaps the only way humanity will ever know what was meant when Jesus Christ said, *"On earth as it is in heaven."*

# Wosapa – blackness

written after the fire

Wosapa - blackness
They all got out
The last one exited the front door
Then wosapa – blackness

Crackling floor
Breaking windows
It happened so fast
The most important things
Walked out
But I couldn't see
Wosapa – blackness

I'm grateful I was awake
I will never again complain
About the strange hours of a crisis counselor
But I couldn't see
And like so many times before
I thank God for guiding me
Through the wosapa - the blackness

# The Cool Kid's Table

The table for the cool kids never enticed me
Clawing their way to wear the prettiest mask
Then looking down on those whose masks
weren't perfected in whatever image deemed cool

Authorities in trends
Rejecting matters of the heart
Grouping together
Defending and attacking
Always at war
Building walls to protect the ever-changing status quo
Of titles, illusion, and ego

At those tables there is no game of truth or dare
Only dare if you will
To share a different view
And if you do, those at the cool kid's table
Gasp, holding their breath,
waiting for the appointed ones
to determine everything,

even their own thoughts

Rejection is seen as death

But what eludes them

Is the moment

They were handed a mask

Their golden ticket for access to this table

They were already rejected

And so they fight to keep it

# When They Called Out to You

Withdrawing into silence, they said it
Numbing it with drugs and alcohol, they said it
The tears they cried said it
The rage they displayed told it
The cuts they made showed it
But what did you hear?

When they called out to you
You called them antisocial and addicts
When they called out to you
You called them weak
When they called out to you
You called them angry
When they called out to you
You called them promiscuous and prostitutes
When they called out to you
You called them psychotic and gang members
When they called out to you
You called them bad and dangerous

You called them many things
But you didn't answer their call
When they called out to you

What you called them when they called out to you
In some ways is easier to deal with
Than the pain they've been through
Wearing your labels like a straitjacket
Holding it together
In summers filled with cold
Holding it all in
Because of what you called them
When they called out to you

For some who eventually broke the rules
Of don't talk, don't tell, and don't feel
Talking, telling, and feeling
At first seems surreal
Voices shaking
Tears streaming
Pain screaming
Releasing what's been broken
Breaking down to a breakthrough
Breaking free from straitjackets
Of what you called them
When they called out to you

With more courage than you'll ever know
They broke free

From what you called them
When they called out to you
With more courage than you'll ever know
They're talking, telling, feeling and healing
And when they do
Some of you call them liars
Some of you say you never knew
But now it doesn't matter what you call them
Because they're no longer
Calling out to you

They're now too busy doing
What you couldn't or wouldn't do
They're answering the calls from others
Responding to pain with love
From those you'd never listen to

But let's give credit where credit is due
You taught them something
You taught them what not to do
By what you called them
When they called out to you

# The Rose is Humble

The rose in full bloom
Nourished when open
Magnificence displayed
Never deciding against itself
The rose is humble

# Time Will Tell

Time will tell
What we tell time
To tell about us

Tales told through time
About what others
Told time to tell
About them

A sprinkle in eternity
To leave a tale
About what you
Told time to tell
About you

Nothing can stand the test of time
Because time is not a test
It's a guest
Welcomed by spiritual beings
Choosing a human experience
For a time
Until time blends back to eternity

# You Can Never Hurt Me

I won't plead, beg, or cry
And I may never know why
Because every conversation I've tried to have
To bridge the divide by opening my heart
Has not been reciprocated
So I will ask no more questions
I will continue to stand with God
In the honor I live
Knowing the truth
About the good man, father, husband
and human being I am
No matter how you choose to see or not see me

Because you see
In the face of lies, disrespect and rejection
Is when I took a ride deep inside
My beautiful heart that God created
And began to live from there
So external validation or permission from others
To see, know, and love myself is not required
Because like you, him, her, they, them
Like everyone else
I am perfectly imperfect

And it took me a long time
To know, love, and like myself
So I'm not going to waste time
Trying to convince anyone else
About the true love I found
Deep within my heart

But it is love because it's without conditions
And we can only offer what's truly within us
So I gave myself permission to live the love I am
And therein lies the secret, and the secret is this -
You can never hurt me
because I will always love you

# Trapped in Time

For so long he felt nothing
Dreams crystallized like shadows
Of what once was
After a nuclear explosion
Frozen in a moment
Looping thoughts
Looping tears
Looping questions
Without answers

Trapped in a time called two
Trapped in a time called eight
Trapped in a time called ten
Trapped in a time called twelve
Trapped in a time called sixteen
Trapped in a time
Within his mind

Shaking hands at funeral parlors
Hearing them say, "I'm sorry"
Isn't what he wanted to hear
And it isn't what they wanted to say
What he wanted to hear
And what they wanted to say is,
"Wake up. It's just a bad dream
Your father, dad, grandparents,
cousin, and brother,
Are in the kitchen laughing and eating
Your best friend hasn't withdrawn
To a place of no return

It's over now
It's all good now"

And if they did say those things
There was a time he would have believed them
A time before being trapped in moments
Of crystallized shadows
In his mind

With each message of love
Every hug of truth
The crystallized shadows melt to tears
From the little boy within him
Bringing back a smile of hope
And life's laughter
The great purification that frees us
From being trapped in time
To live again

# Laughter's Translation

Your being vibrates with sacred tones
Sounds of love that created you
A spark of beginning
In a word!

You came forth
From love-speak
This is your beginning and your understanding
All else is but a distraction
In a word you are created
In a word your true self is revealed and remembered
In a word called love you're here
And yet your Source
is beyond words

Trace the laughter back
Until you remember Laughter's translation
Until you remember Laughter's Source

Wounded one,
Remember what's beyond words
Remember that which is just beyond
The spoken or written
Because in a tsunami of sacred laughter
Air, fire, water, earth become one
Moving us beyond what's beyond words
To know the beauty of you
And God Who created you
In the exquisite perfection you are

In
Heartfelt laughter bringing cleansing tears
To say what no words can
We remember
We just want to laugh with God again

# I'm Somewhere

I'm somewhere
Looking at points in reflections
Cascades of thoughts
Getting lost in my words
Until they find me again
Delivering me gently downstream
To a place of stillness and peace
That I used to feel so much more

Handling broken pieces for a living
I forget to check on me
I forget to listen for the sounds
Of my own heart breaking
I neglect to see my own bleeding
While bandaging others
On a battlefield I've never left

But I'm somewhere
Looking at points in reflections
Cascades of thoughts
Getting lost in my words
Until they find me again
Delivering me gently downstream
To a place of stillness and peace
That I used to feel so much more

# Cravings

If we want our young people to develop an appetite

For love, peace, and compassion

We must first prepare and serve these meals to them

From within the kitchen of our own hearts

Because we cannot crave something

We have never tasted

# A Writer's Courage

A writer's words mean everything to them

Knowing their words will mean nothing to some

Writers cast their pearls

Is there anything more courageous than offering your
heart to this world?

# Orphans Who Were Never Orphaned

In a monastery a group of monks sat and discussed their concerns that the teachings they share seem to be misinterpreted by some who have come to the monastery as a place of refuge.

For centuries people have sought the monastery as a place of refuge to awaken to their highest callings. It's a monastery where all who enter are welcomed, given food, clothing, love, compassion, community, and most importantly, a home. Yet, for the past several years many who came there, even though they did obtained enlightenment, when they left the monastery, they sought to get, not give. Some left and gave themselves titles such as master, monk, teacher, or spiritual leader. Others left and opened up schools where instead of freely giving what was freely given to them, they charged exuberant fees. Because of the many who left the monastery seeking money, titles, and recognition, the monks became perplexed and began to question the manner in which they shared their teachings, because it seemed to not be producing the results of pure selflessness within everyone who departed from there.

Amongst themselves they questioned, "What could be the problem?"

The eldest monk inquired, "Who are the ones that have left here and not given themselves titles or started businesses to make money from that which was freely given to them? Who are the ones that are simply serving others by giving food, clothes, shelter, and most importantly, transmitting love by connecting with those they serve?"

The other monks informed the eldest that the only ones who are out in the community freely giving as was freely given to them are those who came to the monastery as orphans.

"Only the orphans?" Inquired the eldest monk. "We have had many come to us with immense amounts of education. We have had many who come here and understand, articulate, and converse about the deeper aspects of spiritual principles. Many have come here from great amounts of comfort and wealth. Surely it cannot only be the orphans who are the only ones freely giving as was freely given to them."

The other monks assured the eldest that it is indeed only the orphans who continue to live the spiritual principles and enlightenment they obtained while staying at the monastery. Upon hearing this, the eldest monk asked the others to go throughout the monastery, nearby towns, and villages to gather all those who have come to the monastery as orphans. "Please ask them to meet with me near the garden of the monastery at sunrise."

The following morning at sunrise, the eldest monk walked out to the garden of the monastery. Standing around the garden were hundreds of people who were dropped off at the monastery as orphans. Looking out upon them, he became overwhelmed with gratitude and thanked them for meeting with him. He thanked them for carrying on the teachings of love, compassion, and peace by giving freely as was given to them. Still perplexed that the only ones giving freely as was freely given to them were the orphans, the eldest monk asked, "I want to know why the only ones who are carrying on the teachings by freely giving as was given to them are you, you who were once orphans?"

No one said a word. The entire crowd just smiled at the eldest monk like they always do when they are in his presence. After a pause, hoping someone would answer, the eldest monk continued, "I am questioning that perhaps we are not teaching in a manner conducive for true learning if others are not learning truly."

From within the middle of the crowd a nine-year-old girl politely made her way to the front. She lives at the monastery and has since she was four years old. When he saw her step forward, the eldest monk smiled, "Natsuko, do you have some insight about my question?"

Natsuko shared, "Friend, when I was abandoned and had nowhere to go you took me in. I traveled for many days in the cold. When I arrived here at the monastery in the middle of the night, I was cold, hungry, and tired. You woke up when I knocked at the door. Without any hesitation you welcomed me, sat me by the fire, and offered me food. The other monks brought me warm clothes, and you all gave me a room with other girls who came here just like I did. You gave me the name Natsuko which means Summer Child. You said that you gave me my name because even though I came here in the middle of winter on one of the coldest nights, I brought summer with me because the light within me is like a beautiful fire that brings summer wherever it goes. You saw what others couldn't see. You saw me. And because you did, I could see myself."

The eldest monk began to weep, "Natsuko, why doesn't everyone fully receive and give love?"

"Friend, do not weep. This isn't a sad moment. This is a happy moment. When I first came here, I was an orphan and had nothing. I had nothing to gain and nothing to lose. I had no agenda and no motive other than not wanting to die of hunger and cold. I was rejected and no one would help me. Then you welcomed me, clothed me, fed me, and most importantly, you saw me so I could see myself. Remember when I tried to call you *master*?"

"Yes," replied the eldest monk through a smile.

"So do I. And you told me that I can call you friend, uncle, father, brother, but not master, monk, or leader. You told me that all are equal because love created us all equally miraculous. And when you told me to pray and meditate about taking the seventeen-inch walk from my head to my heart and reconnect with the equal blessing, miracle and gift that we all are, I was afraid. I was frightened because of the experiences I had of being rejected by others. Yet, I prayed and meditated and I was taken to the moment when I was born. I was back within the warmth of my mother's womb and being birthed into this life. I was naked, cold and crying. I was wrapped in a blanket and given milk. I was being comforted, nourished, and loved, even if just for a moment.

After that experience I was able to recognize that I was reborn here with a welcoming smile, food, clothing, shelter and love. Oh, how fortunate I am to have once been an orphan so that I could be more open to be reborn through love, because now all I seek is to allow love to birth through me to others. A rebirth through love offered in eye contact, a smile, hug, food, water, clothes or a blanket without ever needing a title. Just knowing that birth and rebirth can happen to all of us throughout the only lifetime that matters - this lifetime.

In some ways we who were once orphans, but no longer are because of the love you and this monastery offer, are more willing to go back to our hearts. Our hearts are all we had when we arrived. Our hearts were the only door we had left that were open to us. And we walked back inside our hearts because you opened your heart to us.

As for the others, if titles, money, and fame are what they seek, may they have them in abundance. May it fill them and make them happy. And if those things leave them orphaned, may the love and teachings they received from here illuminate the path back to what will never abandon them, their hearts. I am grateful they were never orphaned, yet I am also grateful that I was. In being abandoned I was able to go back to and live from what can never abandoned me and so I freely offer it to others – my heart.

Friend, your love helped us to know that we were orphans who were never orphaned, because love won't ever leave us."

# Circular Firing Squad

An army of unwholesome reasoning

Wearing medals of self-righteous indignation

Carrying rifles of unskillful desires

Locked & loaded with bullets of cognitive dissonance

The circular firing squad is ready

# The Most Significant Journey

The most significant journey we can take in this life

Is only seventeen inches

We make this journey by holding hands

With Love, Prayer, Laughter and Tears

Allowing them to walk us

From our head back to our heart

# Until

Until someone can see you as a sacred blessing,
miracle and gift, they cannot see you

# Don't Deny the Light

Don't deny the light you prayed for

Just because you don't like the lamp

That was chosen to bring it

# Believe it

You have been told you are wonderful

And I am concerned

You are not

Starting

To

Believe

It

# Branded

Branded like livestock
An illusion of freedom
Only because the fence is big
Yet there's still that border
Telling us to stay
And only stray
If who branded us
Says it's okay

Teenagers creating art on the streets
With more skills than Picasso
Yet they're branded as criminals
By those holding the branding iron
And the sheeple follow suit
Because sheeple wait for the brander's approval

The old man with wine on his breath
Who had nothing left
But said things more profound
And poetic than any author I've read
Yet he's branded a drunk
So the sheeple don't hear him
The sheeple hear who's branded

As sophisticated and wise
In the brander's eyes

The warrior I knew couldn't read or write
But he could read people
And tell you what
Tomorrow's weather will be like
Based on the sky tonight
He always saw what others missed
Still he's branded as uneducated
By branders afraid of his gift

# Dear Child of God

Dear child of God,

Be blessed by being a blessing to others

Listen to your divine navigational system

Where your dreams take you to is uncertain
Where your dreams take you from
Is the certain suffering of not following them

Right now, in this holy instant
Make the corrections you need to make
And assume your path
You are only seventeen inches away
From your highest callings –
The distance from your head back to your heart

Reclaim your vision, mission
Dreams and purpose
Break through to the real you
The you who knows what I am saying is true

The real you, eternally connected to God
The real you who knows
In this holy instant you can reclaim
All that's within your heart
And soar on your path
The real you who is free
From the illusions of doubt and fear

The real you who knows the answer
When God asks you, "Who are you?"

And you answer by touching your heart
Remembering you never had to become
Because you eternally are

# Let Them Talk

A boy went to a community meeting with his grandfather. The boy loved spending all the time he could with his grandfather because their time together was filled with great stories, laughter and wisdom. Before sitting down at the meeting, the boy and his grandfather helped themselves to some hot chocolate and doughnuts.

During the meeting a man began to talk very badly about the grandfather. The grandfather was simply looking at the man who was speaking ill of him and smiling, until he noticed his grandson had tears streaming down his face.

"Why are you crying, Grandson?"

"Because he's talking bad about you."

"Are the things he is saying about me true?"

"No, and that's why I'm crying."

"So, because he is saying these things about me, does that make them true?"

"No, that's why I'm crying. All you do is help people, and they still talk like that about you."

"Grandson, don't cry for me, cry for him."

"Grandpa, I don't understand."

"I'm helping him right now. He obviously has a lot of anger he needs to get out, and I am happy to help him this way, too. He is speaking volumes about himself and nothing about me or you."

"So what do we do, Grandpa?"

"Enjoy our hot chocolate and doughnuts, and let them talk."

# Rejection Has Its Gifts

You can't uninvite the uninvited
Rejection has its gifts
Like it not affecting you anymore
And when that last hit comes
You no longer strive, chase, plead or beg
You just accept yourself and know
Rejection is impossible when you love and embrace
The you who is eternally connected to the love
That holds it all together when you're falling apart

# People Never Change

People change, growing older
Wearing out earth robes like an old coat
That's seen many winters
Somewhere on the journey we slip out of it
Exchanging it for spirit

People never change
Spirit eternal wrapped in an earth robe
Awakenings to vision like the sun
Rising and setting in the middle of temporary
We see how it shines brighter than all that changes
Because our essence never will

# When That's the Call We Make

It's always a judgement call
When that's the call we make
Speed dial condemnation
And it answers
With an echo of our own voice
Bouncing back through the receiver
We become the receiver
Of all the calls we make

It's always a love call
When that's the call we make
Speed dial forgiveness
And it answers
With an echo of our own voice
Bouncing back through the receiver
We become the receiver
Of all the calls we make

## Beware When the Makeup Artists
## Invite You in Their Chair

So you've made up your mind
That you don't like him or her, they or them
Because you heard something
Because they said, she said, he said
Some call them character assassins
But they're just makeup artists

Character cannot be assassinated
Character is who we are, not what's said
Reputations are merely opinions
And truth is far from the booths
Of makeup artists

The makeup artists say,
"Sit down. Get comfortable."
Then they ask, "Wanna know what I heard?"
If you answer yes then the makeover begins
Gossip, juicy, and compelling
Yet, what are they selling?
And what are you buying into?

Perhaps someone's past
That has nothing to do with them today

Or a good girl who is now a slut
Not in actuality but in your mind
After it was made up
With makeup
From the makeup artists

A good person
Who you had positive experiences with
Becomes bad during your makeover
Friends become foes
Rumors become truth
All in the booth
Of the makeup artists

Makeovers leaving a changeover
A takeover in whispers and online posts
Spreading hurt, lies, gossip, and pain
Having a new disdain for others
Some you've never met
All from one visit to the makeup artists

The victims of the makeup artists
Those who you now hate and berate
For no other reason
Other than what you heard

Sit and wonder why
Then cry as they sit and stare
At a messages you and others left there
There on a text
There online
There inside their mind
Hurtful words that may be absurd
Yet you share them
Only because you heard them
While sitting in the chair of makeup artists

What about the suicides
Of those who couldn't take the pain of words?
Not because those words were true
But because those words came through you
From the booth of the makeup artists

The makeup artists
Changing the way you look at someone
Then everything about that someone changes
Not in truth but through the lens you use
A new perception turns into a projection
Of made up reflection with no introspection
Because your mind was made up with makeup
By the makeup artists

And after you leave the makeup artist's booth
Their next customer gets a makeover
Making up their mind about you
And they leave the booth
Saying their mind is made up
And it is
Made up with makeup
Applied from tongues and whispers like fangs
From the makeup artists
Who are always ready to rearrange
Our thoughts about ourselves and one another

I'm not here to makeup minds
I'm here to remind you of what you'll find
Beyond the makeup of the past or opinions
Because no matter what you say
Or think about me
I will continue to see you
As the blessing, miracle, and gift
You've always been and will always be
In order for both of us to be free
From the makeup artist's chair

The only time we've made up our minds
Is when we find ourselves walking the line

From our minds to our hearts
Then bringing back what's there to share
Once again seeing ourselves and others
In truth only available outside the booth
Of makeup artists

We are sacred, miracles, blessings and gifts
All other perceptions are truly worthless
Because anything less
Is a reflection that our mind was made up
Altered from its original make up
Of divinity, love, compassion and care
So beware when the makeup artists
Invite you in their chair

# The Mirage of the Ego

Two lonely, tired, and thirsty egos met at a cool spring
in the middle of the desert.
The spring was surrounded with a thick layer of rose
petals for weary travelers to sleep upon after they
drank from the pristine water.
The two egos departed from that sacred site together.
Yet, both remained lonely, tired, and thirsty.
Because all they could see was each other.

# The Voice

In 1991 I was driving from Arizona back to Michigan
I was 19 years old but felt like 80
Tired from funerals
Fatigued from running from myself
Crying out for a sign
Somewhere on a stretch of highway
In the New Mexico desert
I saw an eagle swoop down
Pick up a rattlesnake
And fly into the sunset

At that moment, for the first time in a long time,
I heard the Voice
The Voice that consoled me as a child
The Voice that rocked me to sleep
in hospital waiting rooms and rehabs
The Voice that sang to me
when glass broke and adults screamed
Yes! The Voice I thought left me
returned in that moment
Or I returned to it
Either way we celebrated our reunion
By pulling the car over

On the side of the highway
Watching, remembering, knowing
The Sacred will take the poisons
To the Light and purify our plight
Transforming darkness to light
Turning our weakness to might
So we can once again take flight
On the gentle wings of the Voice
Inside our hearts

# We Are Always Faithful

It's impossible to lack faith
Yet we can choose where we would have it be
Faithlessness isn't a lack of faith
But faith in nothing
Faith given to illusions does not lack power
Faith given to illusions turns our power
to powerlessness
Making us faithless to ourselves
Making our faith strong in the illusion
That we are something other than a child of God
And something less
than a sacred blessing, miracle, and gift

# Do We Really See?

Do we really see?

If we really knew what they've been through

We wouldn't condemn them

If we really knew how far they've come

We wouldn't judge them

If we really knew each other's stories

We would celebrate each other

Seeing victory, triumph and God

In ourselves and all those around us

That we really don't see

Until we really do

# Your Blessings, Miracles and Gifts

When you feel unworthy of a blessing
Accept it anyway

When you feel underserving of a miracle
Welcome it anyway

When you feel unmerited of a gift
Receive it anyway

Blessings, miracles and gifts
Often appear when
You feel unworthy
To remind you
That you are worthy

Your blessings, miracles, and gifts
are never just for you

When you receive them, you accept them
for those they are supposed to get to
through you

# Breadcrumbs

Allow your words to be like a trail off breadcrumbs

That inspires the lost, feeds the hungry,

and guides others back to their own hearts

# A Lifetime of Gratitude

A boy and his grandfather were driving down a road on their way to purchase a new fishing pole. They came to a stop sign; the grandfather stopped the truck, looked both ways and was ready to accelerate. Right before the grandfather accelerated the truck to go about their day, he heard his grandson say, "By the grace of God there go I." Upon hearing his grandson say those words the grandfather put his foot back on the brake, looked at his grandson and asked, "What made you say that, Grandson?"

The boy pointed to the corner of the intersection and said, "Over there, Grandpa."

The grandfather looked and saw a man who was holding a sign that read: Homeless. Please Help.

The grandfather immediately pulled the truck over, stared at the man on the corner, and silently contemplated this moment with his grandson. As the grandfather stared at the man, the grandson was watching his grandfather with great anticipation of what was stirring within the thoughts of his grandfather. The boy knew his grandfather always seemed to seamlessly take what was around him, blend it with his lifelong experiences, and unfolded a precious gift of wisdom that the elders so graciously carry.

"Grandson, let's go."

"Go where, Grandpa?"

"We're going over there to that man, because we both need to reintroduce ourselves to him."

Excited about the impromptu journey, the boy exclaimed, "You know him?"

"Yes, and you know him, too. Moments like these are an important opportunity to know him even more."

Hurriedly the boy got out of the truck. Side by side, the grandfather and his grandson walked over to the man who had just been given a couple of dollars from a passerby in a vehicle. The man looked at the elder and boy with surprise and confusion, but didn't say a word. The grandpa smiled and said, "Hello. My name is Earl and this is my grandson Tommy."

Reluctantly the man extended his hand and shook Earl and Tommy's hands sharing, "My name is Mark. I'm not trying to be rude, but I don't have many people coming up to me out here, so what do you want?"

Through his smile Earl replied, "We want to know you, so we came over here to introduce ourselves."

Trying to read the intentions of the grandfather and grandson, Mark cautiously answered, "Okay, well, nice to meet you both."

With the gentleness of a loving grandfather, Earl extended his hand again towards Mark, but this time within Earl's hand he had a folded fifty-dollar bill that he was going to use to buy the new fishing pole. Mark, not seeing the money in Earl's hand, and perhaps a little at ease because the boy was there, reciprocated and loosely gripped Earl's hand again. With a tender grip, and never breaking eye contact with Mark, Earl said, "It is an honor to know you. You are a blessing, miracle, and gift." Connected with one another, hand in hand, Earl felt the subtle shutter that rose from somewhere deep within Mark when those words were spoken. Earl gently released his hand from Mark's hand as the fifty-dollar bill lightly fell into Mark's palm. Mark looked in his hand and saw the money he was gifted with. Bewildered and through teary eyes Mark sniffled, "Thank you for the money, but I don't know why you're saying these things to me. You have no idea where I'm from, what I've done, or what I'm going to do with the money you just gave me."

With great love and conviction Earl responded, "Mark, we are from the same place. Anything you've done doesn't change what you are, which is a blessing, miracle, and gift. Whatever you do with the money is your business, but the chances of you using it in a manner that will help you instead of hurt you are greater when you know the real gift is you, not what we gave you. We are happy to know you. It is our honor to know you, and if we see you out here again, I hope you don't mind if we visit some more."

The street armor Mark had to wear due to the circumstances he lived in every day melted in the presence of the love that exuded from Earl. Mark embrace Earl and Tommy with a warm hug of gratitude. Through his tears Mark cried, "Thank you both so much. You have no idea how much I needed this today, and I'm not talking about the money."

After their embrace, Mark stepped back and looked at Earl and his grandson with eyes transformed from hardened suspicion to the indomitable strength that only exists within the tenderness of love. In a brief moment of silence Mark and Earl smiled and nodded an unspoken, yet understood agreement to one another. Earl gently took his grandson's hand and they walked back to their vehicle and got back inside the truck.

Before starting the truck, Earl looked at his grandson who was staring out of the passenger's window and asked, "So what do you think, Grandson?"

"I'm confused, Grandpa. You said you knew him. You said we knew him, and we were going to reintroduce ourselves to him."

"Yes, I said that, so what are you confused about?"

"We didn't even know his name, and he didn't know ours. As a matter of fact, he looked nervous when we first walked up to him because he didn't know us."

"Grandson, when we pulled up to the stop sign and you saw Mark from the truck, what was it you said?"

"By the grace of God there go I."

"Why did you say that?"

"Because when someone is in a position that's tough, that saying reminds me that if it wasn't for the grace of God, I could be the person in that position. It reminds me to be grateful for my life, and that I do have it better than some other people."

"Grandson, true gratitude isn't found in the suffering of others but in alleviating the suffering of others. Who is it that you think you just met?"

"Mark."

"No, we were reintroduced to God and to ourselves. Mark is a part of God, a part of us. The next time you see someone suffering, instead of saying by the grace of God there go I, consider saying by the grace of God there goes God, and then reintroduce yourself to God, yourself, your relative, and true gratitude."

"Grandpa, if I did that every time I saw someone suffering I would be doing that for the rest of my life."

"Grandson, that would be a life well lived, because that would be a lifetime of gratitude."

# Discernment of the Eagle

The eagle is unwilling

To pick up a wounded rattlesnake

Take it back to its nest

And nurse the rattlesnake back to health

The rattlesnake yells, "You're judgmental!"

The eagle goes gracefully about its day

Unaffected by the words

Of a predator

# Without Definitions

What doesn't define me
Sets me free
What doesn't define me
Makes me us
Whole-holy-one

Without separation
Without without
From within I write
Knowing it's a glimpse
Of what we can't grasp
But what we are
What used to be
All we know
I'm writing to forget
Everything
That makes me forget

Like eagles
Flying until they're done
Not knowing or caring
How we define them
They know we're one
They soar
Without defining
They soar within
What can't be defined

To those called fools
Who flushed rules with their stool

And moved beyond measurements
To remember truth is not defined
And there is no bottom line
You're my heroes
The rest of us are awakening
To what's beyond definitions

Let me be the uneducated
Bumblebee I am
Knowing not physics
I've heard colors
I've seen sounds
I've flown
And I'm not alone

Don't educate me
Label me
Or define me
Just remind me
Of the us
We knew so well
Before definitions confined my curiosity
And vanquished me to hell

Don't define me
Set me free
Don't define me
Remind me
That you are me
So we can soar
Without definitions

# The Beams You Hid From Me

The splinters in my eyes
That you didn't even see
I pointed out to you
For us to be free

In time
You would have seen my mistakes
And realize I can't fit
In superhero capes

Jumping off the cliff of fear
Landing in vulnerability
Swimming in authenticity
I welcomed you inside my heart

I forgot about my splinters
And didn't see me as a mistake
But one day everything changed
Like a bad dream
From which I couldn't wake

All you saw were my splinters
And each day they grew
Not in actuality
But within the lens
You saw me through

You changed the way you looked at me
So everything about me changed

My splinters became beams to you
Then nothing was the same

For many years I looked at me
Through the lens you used
It made me hate myself
Feeling worthy of being abused

There was something in your eyes
That drove you to see
The splinters in my eyes
It was the beams you hid from me

## God's Refrigerator

Stop painting pictures of other people

Wake up every day

and paint a better picture of yourself

So God can hang it on His refrigerator

# The Right Intention in Youth Gang Intervention

Originally published in Red Man Films

The wounds within gang life are small compared to the wounds that cause our young people to choose a life within gangs. Yes, there are some things worse than death in this life. All healthy relationships begin with the ability to open our hearts without fear of being hurt. And healthy relationships end when we can no longer open our hearts with someone due to the anticipation of pain. Gang affiliation is one of many cloaks some young people turn to after their hearts close due to pain. After the light that our young people brought to contribute to this life is rejected one too many times by those who are supposed to support them, some youth hide it under gang affiliation. Gang affiliation is not the problem, but a symptom of many problems. And when we identify any young person as a gang member, what is really being identified is great pain.

I was once asked, "Don't you ever get tired of working with gang members?" I responded, "If that's how I saw them I probably would." The irony of facilitating successful gang intervention is this: First, don't see the youth as gang members, even if that's what they present, and continue to represent. See them as what they are, Wakanyeja (Sacred Beings), gifts, miracles. Remember that the gang clothing, and hand signs are just there to throw you off, and perhaps test you to see if you will fall for the thin disguise they picked up to mask the pain they endured. Will you continue to see the light within them, or focus on the street armor many young people wear due to not wanting to be hurt again?

For twenty-one years now I've been blessed to work with what some label as "high risk youth." High risk youth are equally at high certainty of a great healing and transformation. Miracles are not beyond anyone, they're within everyone. I've been to more gang conferences than I can remember. In many gang conferences and workshops I've attended most of the people adorned the title of *gang expert* is due to being able to tell you everything there is to know about gang identification in terms of clothing, hand signs, graffiti, etc. This may be useful in law enforcement practice, but if your calling is to facilitate healing with our young people, what you need is the only thing that can penetrate the street armor without harming anyone - love.

Yes, I said it, love, and I've been criticized countless times by law enforcement minded individuals and groups for it. I've heard all the clichés such as, "Oh here comes the hug-a-thug approach guy." Trust me, I think nothing of these critiques, our calling is too great, and the lives of our youth are on the line, so there's no time for ego-stench. Gang affiliated youth are constantly thrown into the categories of unreachable and un-teachable by many people in our society. No one is unreachable or un-teachable as long as the heart doing the reaching and teaching is full of love, honor, and respect.

Facilitating healing with the youth has nothing to do with blame, it's about walking them back to where pain and blame took them from, their hearts. Unfortunately, a not so uncommon mantra from unskilled, unseasoned, or uncalled youth workers is, "Those kids are going to have to earn my respect!"

Let me break this down:

1. If you have to demand respect, it's not respect.
2. If you see our youth as sacred, what's there not to respect?
3. Correcting unacceptable behavior is effectively done with respect.
4. Recognizing the pain behind the behavior is only seen with eyes of love and respect.
5. If it's not unconditional love and respect, then it's not love and respect.
6. If love and respect are not the foundation of the work with our youth, it's not youth work.
7. Put that ego away before you hurt someone.

Regardless of the choice of curriculums and approaches utilized to facilitate gang intervention, the level of effectiveness always stems from the intention from which it's delivered. Facilitate everything with love and respect in order for our youth to remember they're sacred by being treated as such. Our youth are not lost, their greatness just got lost in the pain. As we facilitate healing with love and respect, we remember our own sacredness as well, which in turn makes the youth our teachers. When we're willing to learn from our young people they're willing to learn from us.

# That's All I Will Ever Be

*That's all you will ever be*
They sang to me
With persistence, conviction and consistency

In the darkness of my cocoon
I heard them but couldn't see
I looked for light and found it
Inside of me

The light said,
"Join the chorus of that's all you will ever be
To ensure you never get to those
Who you were sent to help see"

Knowing I was scared and doubting
The light spoke again,
"My instructions to you will only make sense
After you're free, my friend"

With a deep breath I twisted and turned
My wings began to grow
Growing pains hurt but the torture of their song
I no longer wanted to know

The more I focused on the light inside of me
The louder they sang
*That's all you will ever be*

My wings grew larger
Cracking my cocoon
The light once only inside me
Now filled my room

The last fragments of my cocoon
Flew away from me
The light was everywhere and in everyone
I could see

Now outside of my cocoon
The light again spoke,
"The song of that's all you will ever be
Was never sung to you but often is to me"

I looked upon the majestic field of life
Countless butterflies who are free
Yet their eyes closed tight
Not believing the light
Their own exquisiteness they refuse see

Perfect butterflies sit paralyzed by lies
Where their cocoons used to be
Trapped in a moment of darkness
By continually singing
*That's all I will ever be*

# Make Your Mind a Demilitarized Zone

Originally published in Elephant Journal

One of my first mentors told me, "Whatever you embark upon, the goal is always peace." My mentor did not come from some isolated, sheltered background where he never experienced hurt, pain, loss, and trauma. He came from every conceivable form of violence imaginable, and because he experienced the opposite of peace for so long, he understood the significance of peace more than some. The challenge is that even when we know and lived the exact opposite of peace and have come through our struggles and want to help, we can bring a warlike mindset to healing work. A warlike mindset will not produce healing, only confusion, and when people are confused they tend to go to what is comfortable and understood even if it's not what they truly want. In order for us to not bring confusion to the healing work we do it is imperative that we continually ensure that our mindset is a demilitarized zone where peace dwells, is cultivated and shared.

Our mind's zone is truly within our full control regardless of any outside circumstances. We as humanity will not know peace until we first know it within our minds. The challenge for so many is that although people often say they want peace, their mind continues to be a militarized zone that is always attacking or defending, and seeking better ways to improve this cycle from the perceived enemy. What if the entire lifespan of a militarized mind is the enemy that is not only being harbored by us, but is a most vicious dictator that is running and ruining our true growth as a human being?

Messengers from all cultures and religions have stated in one form or another that when there are rumors of war, and talk of war, a war is coming. Understand that what they shared with all of us is that there cannot be rumors and talk without the thoughts first. Warlike thoughts produce warlike language, which will ultimately result in a reality – a reality of war. If we truly want peace, then we have to be clear that peace is also a reality, a reality that first begins within our thoughts. When we hear talk and rumors of peace, rest assured that it will ultimately result in a reality – a reality of peace.

In a demilitarized mind you will not allow others to house weapons of mass destruction such as gossip, contrived malice, prejudice, discrimination, unwholesome thoughts, and unskillful desires. Within the gardens of a demilitarized mind exists appreciative inquiry, respect, patience, compassion, empathy, understanding, and love.

A militarized mind will hit the panic button either declaring an emergency lockdown or a full-scale attack over differences in opinions and perspectives. A demilitarized mind knows that different opinions are wonderful, and there is no attack or defense needed, and surrender to another's views are never expected because surrender only happens in war. A mind that is a demilitarized zone is not interested in being right, but in understanding. Missed understandings (misunderstandings) are missed opportunities to cultivate peace, which is why listening from the heart will awaken heart-language and true dialogues, not monologues.

In a demilitarized zone your meetings with yourself and others will not be discussions and plans of character assassination, accusations, competition, defense, and attacks. The meetings will be focused on solutions, collaboration, and looking at how to place differences together like pieces from a jigsaw puzzle to create a beautiful picture. Everyone holds different pieces, but no piece is less necessary or less significant than anyone else's.

Perhaps peace is the greatest gift we are sent to this life to share, and for some, the first thing we forgot. Peace can also be the next thing we remember in this moment, right now. Peace is not a process but a decision. There are only two sides we can take - love or fear. On the side of love is peace and on the side of fear is war. For those who truly want peace, now is the time to demilitarize our internal thought process and allow peace to take over the world within us, then the world outside of us.

# Pebbles and Wrecking Balls

The boomerang came back
A wrecking ball the size of Jupiter
Destroying everything
And the few of us left at laughing, crying,
smoking cigarettes, and thanking the Creator
At ground zero
Then someone appeared and threw a pebble at us
Making us laugh even more
More than a few times my brothers and me laughed
Cried, smoked cigarettes, and thanked the Creator
At ground zero
And more than a few times people threw pebbles at us
Right after a wrecking ball
The size of Jupiter came through
Which made us laugh even more

# The War Behind Your Eyes

You're playing chess
Making all your best moves
Strategizing against me
Thinking eight moves ahead
Dominating the chessboard

After days, months, years
Of your blood, sweat, and tears
You finally get to yell *check mate*!
Then you look across the board
And I'm not there
You were playing yourself
And I hope you won
But I'm over here smiling
Loving you
Praying for you
I have no strategy
I have no secrets
And in a world where vulnerability is so rare
I understand your discomfort
When I just throw my heart on the table for all to see

My heart on my sleeve seems strange to you
Yet what else can I offer you
That's worthy of a child of God?

I've played the games you're playing
That's why I hope you win
Defeat every lie that separates you from you

Then soon you'll see the reason us mad ones
Live with our hearts wide open
Is that there's no safer place
We're invulnerable within what you call vulnerable
Because love has no opposite
Only illusions of opposites
exist within the games you're playing

Keep playing if you must
No rush - take your time
The other mad ones and me will be over here smiling
Loving you
Praying for you
Waiting for the war
That's behind your eyes
To end

# Naive

Voices of fear sweeping voices of love away
into war and hate
Yet when we were young we could clearly see
Love, peace and unity
Then some were swept away
Their true voices taken under the tide
Screaming inside and no one would listen
The voices of fear calling them naive
Ripping them apart with the tides of war to believe

Each night millions recite
*On Earth as it is in Heaven*
Yet are too blind to see
The answer to this prayer has been given
Through the children

The children's natural instincts
of love, peace and unity
Is bombarded with adults who say,
"That's cute but it's naivety
We know the real world, you see"

The children respond,
"Yes, we see, but you no longer do
That's why we're here to remind you
But like adults did with all the prophets before
They were left bloody and dead
Lying on the floor
And you do this to us, too

Attempting to destroy the same message of peace
Someone else destroyed in you

You say you believe you're made
In the likeness and image of God
Yet you make God in the likeness and image of war
And you're trying to do the same to us children
All the while you recite
*On Earth as it is in Heaven*
While calling us - the children
The answers to your prayers
Naive"

# Be In Peace - Stay In Love

Don't be distracted

Cry the tears you need to cry

When you need to cry them

Allow the Creator to fight the battles

Being waged against you

Be in peace

Stay in love

# Too Simple to be Heaven

As the sea reminds us of eternity
The grains of sand are equally certain
Certain in eternity - infinite
Then fear set in and a roadblock to remembrance
Was created

Created from the reminders of eternity
Created from what keeps us humble
Created to create a known
Created to not feel humility -
Gratitude with the Creator

The original dream of paradise wasn't good enough
No place to take pride
Hang a name or have the credit
The enjoyment of bounty, balance and freedom
Wasn't enough
They devised a way to make a need for more
Out of something endless

They took the reminders of sharing and simplicity
They took them from the earth
Mixed them together and began to build
They built, and built, and built
And are still building

It's never enough - enough is contentment
And that's what they're running from
Running from the memory of our oneness

Developing more hurt with more development

Attempting to override destruction
with more construction
Though some still long for the place
of the original dream
Thought, time and space

Those who remember never drank the mix
Longing for what they knew it was
before it was this
Seeing what can be for the future of our children
They see that all the children can have enough

Those who remember
Are called naive and unrealistic
They're told, "Shut up!
It's not the way of the world!"
Heaven whispers,
"It used to be and can be again"
Heaven's whisper is drowned out
with sounds of progress

Coursing through the veins of destruction
A flow of mixture that is always given
enough money to eat
It's always eating and given the priority
It's why money was made
It has become a false god
by those denouncing false gods

Before they used it to cover the earth

Before they used it to encase our children
They drank it deep within their hearts
Devouring cement to devour a memory
That's too simple to be Heaven

# We Can't See Each Other Through Mistakes

Two friends, Mary and Louis decided to meet for dinner. They hadn't had a face-to-face visit for many years, and were both looking forward to the opportunity to catch up with one another. They each brought a letter that they wanted to share over dinner.

Seventeen years ago, Louis had been at one of the lowest points of his life. He went through a rough breakup, addiction, and was in an inpatient rehab clinic for a time due to feeling like his life was meaningless and wanting to end things. While he was in rehab, Mary never gave up on him. Mary and her husband encouraged Louis and visited him often. She had sent him a letter while he was in rehab that changed his life for the better. Louis went on to do some deep work, dove back into a daily prayer life, and decided to use all of his talents for something meaningful. Louis went back to school, completed his degree in radio broadcasting, and was now a very popular radio personality in St. Louis, Missouri. He was doing what he loved and was truly happy. The letter from his friend Mary is what he carried with him to their meeting. Because he wanted to say thank you to her, and remind her of the great significance her words had upon his life. He wanted to share his gratitude.

Mary brought a different kind of letter. She was worried that her friend had become arrogant and felt the need to remind him about where he came from. She took the time to write a seven-page letter reminding him of all of his mistakes. Within the pages of the letter she wrote, contained his struggles with addiction, his bad decisions, the times he sabotaged great opportunities, as well as when he was so low that he wanted to end his own life. She wanted to help him keep his feet on the ground because of his successes. She wanted to share humility.

When the two met for dinner, they embraced in front of the restaurant and looked into one another's eyes. They were genuinely happy to see one another. They went inside the restaurant and were seated at their table. After some formalities, small talk and catching up about their spouses and children, Louis said, "I have a letter with me that I want you to read."

With great surprise Mary exclaimed, "I have a letter I want you to read as well. This is great because there is something I really want to talk with you about. I wrote you a long letter because I love you, and I hope we can talk about it when you're done reading it. But you go first, Louis. I always enjoyed reading the things you wrote."

Pulling the letter from his pocket, Louis shared, "Mary, this isn't a letter I wrote. It's a letter you wrote to me seventeen years ago when I was in that very dark space in my life. I have carried this letter with me every day since you gave it to me. I've went back to this letter more times than I can count to remind myself of what you reminded me of seventeen years ago. I had to read this letter every day for an entire year just to muster up the courage to move on with my life, but I did, and it was because of your words in this letter."

Louis slid the letter across the table to Mary. Mary opened up the seventeen-year-old letter she had forgotten about, but remembered rather quickly when she saw her own handwriting. She read the letter aloud.

*Louis,*
*You are a dear friend to me. And I love you very much. You told me about all the mistakes you've made. I've watched you rise and fall with so many things, but you've never given up. Yes, you have made some bad decisions, but who hasn't? We all have, and we all will again, but we are not our mistakes, so instead of saying "because of" start saying "despite of." You have been saying because of your addiction your life is over. No, despite your addiction God is all powerful, and you can move past this. You've been saying because of your bad choices you are not a good husband for anyone, a good father, a good friend, a good student, or a good employee. No! This is not true! Despite your bad choices you are an excellent husband, father, friend, student and employee. We are not our mistakes! Despite the many times you fell, and you have fallen hard, you are and will always be a miracle, blessing and gift. You are significant to this world, to me, and your family and friends who love you, despite how you see yourself at this moment. You, my friend, are talented, amazing, articulate and have so much to offer this world, and so much to contribute to the great healing this world desperately needs. This world desperately needs you. Today may suck big time, but despite this moment, tomorrow will be better, and it will be so much better for me and many others you haven't even met yet, with you in it,*

*despite your mistakes. The lessons from our mistakes*
*are the blessings of our mistakes to learn from and*
*share with others. You are not your mistakes! You*
*are a child of the Creator! You are a precious*
*miracle, blessing and gift. Anyone who wants to*
*carry your mistakes around for you, well, let them*
*carry them if they want because you carrying them*
*around isn't doing you any good. Only carry the*
*blessed lessons from your mistakes. Move forward in*
*the greatness you are created in. I gratefully look*
*forward to watching God unfold the masterpiece you*
*are, always have been, and always will be.*
*Love,*
*Mary*

After Mary read the letter, she handed it back to
Louis. Neither one of them had noticed they were
served their salads while Mary was reading the letter.
Louis took a bite of his salad and while chewing his
food said, "You said you have a letter you wrote for
me, so now it's your turn." Mary sat across from
Louis, carrying all of the mistakes of her friend in her
purse. In that moment she realized that when we
place ourselves in a position to humble another
person that is perhaps the most arrogant position of
all. Humility comes from the gratitude we carry, not
the mistakes of ourselves or others. Just as Mary had
told Louis seventeen years ago, she now whispered to
herself, "I am not my mistakes." She didn't share the
letter she wrote, but she did receive the blessed
lesson. She excused herself, walked to the bathroom,
and flushed the letter of mistakes down the toilet. She
knew that if she truly wanted to see him, which she
did, she would not be able to while carrying around
his mistakes.

# We Rise In Love
# We Fall In Fear

God asked me, "Will you remember?"
"Of course I will," I answered
With a smile God whispered, "Of course you will"

Nudged out of Spirit World
I flew through my mother
Adjusting to the confinements of body
I tried to crawl and I fell
Learning to balance using my belly arms
and big head
I rose -
I crawled

Crawling to the table, wanting to see
I tried to stand and I fell
Reaching for what was around me
I lifted myself
Learning to balance
My legs shook
Standing for seconds
Then minutes
Eventually I rose -
I stood

Progress!
Oh, the excitement of standing
Made me move towards life
I tried to walk and I fell

Inch by inch from table to chair
And then back again
Learning balance
From room to room
Then outside
Eventually I rose –
I walked

Walking and talking
Feeling like I'm part of this existence
I tried to run and I fell
Walking quickly, looking for balance
In my scraped hands, knees and face
My speed walking and I became one
And it was fun
Eventually I rose -
I ran

I could run
Why would I want to walk?
When I ran I felt like I could fly
For years I fell to fly
Then I saw her, and I fell again
Passing notes and holding hands
Eventually I rose -
I loved

Adults called it puppy love
Yet what I felt made me remember
God's whisper
For years I forgot what I knew

Until I flew -
and love made me rise

Rising to crawl
Walking to run
Each time I rose in love the butterflies in my stomach
Reminded me of my wings -
The feeling love brings

Rise in love!
Fly in love!
Nudged out of the bosom of God
To bring butterflies back to the stomachs of others
So they remember their wings -
The feeling love brings

For a moment I decided against love
Using my wings to reach outside of love -
I fell
And a moment outside of love felt like eternity
Yet it didn't make love less real
With fear my butterflies turned back to caterpillars
I found myself enclosed in a cocoon of fear's cousins -
condemnation, regret and doubt

God unfolded the cocoon of fear so I could see
Looking at me God smiled
The light of God's smile dispelled fear's illusion
God didn't unfold my cocoon
God unfolded my wings!

For a moment I retracted my wings

Wrapped them tightly
Around myself -
And fell in fear

We fall in fear
We rise in love
Every time God asks us, "Will you remember?"
We answer, "Of course I will"
With a gentle smile God whispers,
"Of course you will"

## That's Purification

The young man bowed his head before entering the lodge and introduced himself to the Creator. Inside the lodge the young man asked his uncle, "Uncle, why do I have to introduce myself to the Creator when I enter the lodge? Doesn't the Creator already know who I am?"

Through his laughter the old man shared, "Nephew, of course the Creator knows who you are. You're not reminding the Creator, you're reminding yourself. We come here to remember who we are with the Creator, and rid ourselves of all that makes us forget. That's purification."

# It Wants to Talk With You

The Sacred of sacred

The Holy of holies

Wants to talk with you

To remind you of your greatness

Why do you sit reading negative reviews?

The Sacred of sacred

The Holy of holies

Wants to talk with you

To remind you

You're a

Sacred blessing

Miracle

and

Gift

# An Ancient Approach
# to Relationships & Healing

*An ancient understanding of a successful approach to relationships passed on from the Native American elders of Turtle Island...*

There were three different groups of travelers walking along the same path at different times. Each of the groups of travelers carried offerings with them.

The first group of travelers came upon a tree they recognized as poisonous. Because they recognized the tree contained some poisonous elements, they motioned for everyone to go far around the tree, which they did. The first group of travelers offered *avoidance.*

Days later, the second group of travelers encountered the tree. They, too, recognized the tree contained some poisonous elements. This group saw the tracks of the first group that went far around the tree. The second group of travelers decided to tie a blue cloth to the tree to warn future travelers the tree was poisonous. The second group of travelers offered *labels.*

A week passed when the third group of travelers came into the vicinity of the tree. They saw the tracks that went far around the tree, as well as the blue cloth warning them the tree was poisonous. The third group also recognized the tree contained poisonous elements. But after much prayer and contemplation, the third group of travelers decided to make their camp around the tree. The tree became the center of their camp and they shared an entire season with the tree. They learned the poisons the tree contained could be transformed into healing medicines when cultivated with care, patience and love. The medicine the tree produced cured sicknesses that once had no cure. With honor, they approached the tree, and with equal honor they parted ways with the tree. Before they left, the group sang a thank you song and tied a red cloth under the blue cloth, marking the tree as holy - a significant reminder of the truth that Heaven and Earth are forever connected by the sacredness within all living beings. The third group of travelers offered *relationship*.

Because of the great courage only love can provide, the third group of travelers left tracks many others have been able to follow for healing. Because of love, the tree is no longer avoided or labeled, but sought for its truth of healing.

# What is Arrogance?

I was speaking with Love, and I asked her,
"Love, what is arrogance?"
Love whispered,
"Arrogance is thinking you know more than me"

# Have You Seen Him?

He is a man of valor

He is someone dependable

He is living his dreams and being of benefit to others

He doesn't live his mistakes, but he learns from them

He is gentle, loving, and kind

He is both warrior and poet

His laughter fills rooms and hearts

He is alive – living!

He is every woman's dream

He is every boy's role model

He is every boy

Underneath the pain and scars

Of becoming a man in this society

He is a real man

Unlike what society deems as real

He really is a good man

# Humility

Go sit in the woods alone

For a day or two or four

See how the sun rises and sets

How creation continues

Without you doing what you do

Experience that nothing in creation

Is dependent upon you

To remember that you are dependent

Upon everything within creation

# A Dance Without Love

There we were

Me and him

My opposite and I

Dancing

Until he tried to kill me

I lived

He died

But he was never there

It's a dance with illusion

Whenever we dance without love

# Celestial EKG

Do you know each beat of your heart

Sings I am - I am - I am?

Love wants your mind to fill in what comes after *I am*

With what it knows you to be -

Courageous

A warrior whose love is large enough

to blanket the world

Because once your heart was wrapped in an earth robe

You appeared to remind and remember

Only that which your heart speaks

Love-speak from the depth of

I am - I am - I am

Powerful, courageous, beautiful

Strong, significant, intelligent

A divine spark whose fire lights

ancient, holy memories

A holy memory in a holy instant

You sing with love

Filling the space between heartbeats

With the truth about you

I am - I am - I am Love

That which created you exactly like Itself

Remember how to read

Your celestial EKG

That will never flat line

Within or outside the dimensions of time

Because the love you are is beyond time

and

Timelessness

# My Mother

We've had our ups and downs

Our many times of separation

Our many years of distance

She buried her parents

She buried her in-laws

She buried two husbands

She buried a nephew

And then went through

Everything I put her through when I was a young man

Then there were the other things

It's as if she fought every demon

hell could possibly send

And here she still stands in God's victory

My mother isn't perfect, who is?

But she is my mother

The strongest person I've ever known

And I don't know why she was dealt the hands she was

But she played them all

All in

Never hesitating

She knocked out a woman

Twice her size at a bar

Because the woman

Said something negative about me
So before you judge how someone plays their hands
Remember the cards you got to start with
Because even if they weren't perfect
Chances are they're a hell of a lot better cards
Than the cards those came before you had
A warrior who sacrificed and fought
All the demons hell could send
And for you they never backed down
They stood in courage with God
Until God's victory manifested
Because you, son, daughter, grandson,
granddaughter, niece, nephew -
Are the reason they struggled,
fought and lived

# Leave It Wild

Originally published in Elephant Journal

I would rather have a love that burns it all down

And sit with you in the ashes -

The residue of our passion

Knowing that even if our tracks go different directions

We experienced a fire many try to control

A fire most are too afraid to go near

But we allowed it to consume us

And when we experience a love like this

We no longer fear death

Because for as long as the fire burned, we lived

As others slowly die trying to control

What should be left wild

# The Password is 5683 L-O-V-E

Wouldn't it be cool if we treated our hearts
The way we treat our cell phones?

Checking it first thing in the morning
It being the last thing we look at
before we sleep

Immediately answering its callings
Instantly responding to its messages
Protecting it
Allowing necessary updates to consistently renew it
and rid it of viruses

Always aware of where it is,
what it's doing & the sounds it makes
Putting our whole life in it
Sharing our whole life with it
And even when it's silent, we still check it

At a table with family and friends
We read it aloud
Sharing all that's there
Giving all that is within it
Our friends and family watch out for it
They pick it up if we forget it
And hand it to us with a smile

If we lose it, we thoroughly trace our steps
Back to the last time we held it
We call it

Hoping someone trustworthy answers
and is holding it carefully
Until we are reunited with it and feel a great relief
When it's safely back in our hands

Even when it's broken, we still use it
Peering through what's shattered
To know what's inside
We communicate with it
Until we take it to the Master
Who created it
To renew it
Until it needs to be renewed again

It has a secret password that's not so secret
To unlock all that's within
the place of true selfies
Most precious moments
The beauty of you
The truth that you are
a sacred blessing, miracle and gift
Is behind a password everyone knew well
When we were children
The password is 5683
L-O-V-E

# Hold On

If you feel like you don't belong

Hold on

You'll find it a little beyond this moment

Where there's no longer a longing for belonging

# There's Always a Trace

No one vanishes without a trace
There's always a trace
Within those who love them
Moments others can't see
Scents others can't smell
Laughter others can't hear
Truth others cannot know
And we are acquainted with the traces
of all ancestors
Through each other, to know everyone
Who has ever existed in moments, scents,
laughter and truth

It's easier when someone vanishes away from us
Than when they vanish in front of us
And seem to become someone we no longer know
Perhaps it's most painful when this happens to us
Looking in the wrong mirror
We forget the love we are
Until the holy instant when love reminds us
Of moments, scents, laughter and truth
as your beautiful heart shines away the clouds
From your mind

Illuminating the path of the sacred
And you see all that traces you back to God
In holy instances and holy memory
We know no one vanishes
Without a trace

# On The Razor's Edge

On the edge is where I find myself
It may not make sense to you
But you're not me
And I don't have to be understood to understand
When I find myself on the edge is when I find myself
A razor's edge is where I stand
Reaching a little beyond
Grasping at what has no words
Touching what has no reference
And since it has no reference – it's free
You can't say, "Yeah, it's like..."
Because it's not like anything
Like writing about the sound
Of the color yellow
Bringing other dimensions
To this dimension
Doesn't make the artist crazy
It makes some refer to the artist as crazy
Because the reference of crazy
Is a reference that others create
For those who create something
That has no reference
And are too afraid to walk
The razors edge and float without one
Like the sound of the color yellow

# I Remember Melvin

Waking up again
Middle of the night thoughts
Bringing eyes open
To tears flowing
Not even sure what the dream was about
Crying myself awake
Maybe tears held back
Rain with ease
When we're in that place of dreams
Dreams that came true
Dreams that broke
Some dreams are still in progress
But man, I remember Melvin
A 60 year old
Diagnosed with schizophrenia
Self-medicated with crack rock
And anything else
He could get his hands on
He taught me so much about faith
He taught me so much about God
God spoke through Melvin
Being in Catholic school
Until I got expelled
I must have said the *Our Father*
Thousands of times
But I never prayed it
Until Melvin prayed it with me
I don't know why
I'm writing about Melvin
Maybe it's because

He taught me about faith
During a time
When I lost it
While I was looking to spiritual leaders
Instead of God
And then Melvin said,
"Let's look up, Mr. Tony
And then close our eyes
And look within
Because He still talks to us
And people that listen to Him
Are rarely listened to
By people who only talk about Him"

# Take Your Time

Take your time

As much time as you need

There really is no hurry

And some will only realize this

after there is no more time to take

## Through This Moment

I make better illusions than I used to
Waking up with stardust in my eyes
I can't help it
Love is all I see
Let me dream walk through this moment with you
Hold my hand and don't tell me you're not there

# God's Math

I'm not a theologian nor a mathematician

We know God through love not religion

Love given is only addition

In God's math there exists no division

www.realwarriorslove.com

Made in the USA
Columbia, SC
01 October 2023

23654403R00083